DATE DUE

MAR 2 5 2019			
			PRINTED IN U.S.A.

PERIODS SAY

"STOP."

written by
MICHAEL DAHL

illustrated by
CHRIS GARBUTT

PICTURE WINDOW BOOKS
a capstone imprint

A period is
BUSY.

A period does not
play around.

Periods pop up at the
END of sentences.

The wind howled.
Trees shook and
shadows danced.
The moon hid
behind heavy clouds.

Like me!

Me too!

And me!

A breeze blew. Trees w

Flowers danced in the

was warm and bright.

the top of the hill sat

A period lets you know
when one sentence ENDS
and another BEGINS.

When you see a period, you stop.
Then you go on to the next sentence.

OK, now you may go on.

Thank you for your attention.

WATCH OUT for more periods.

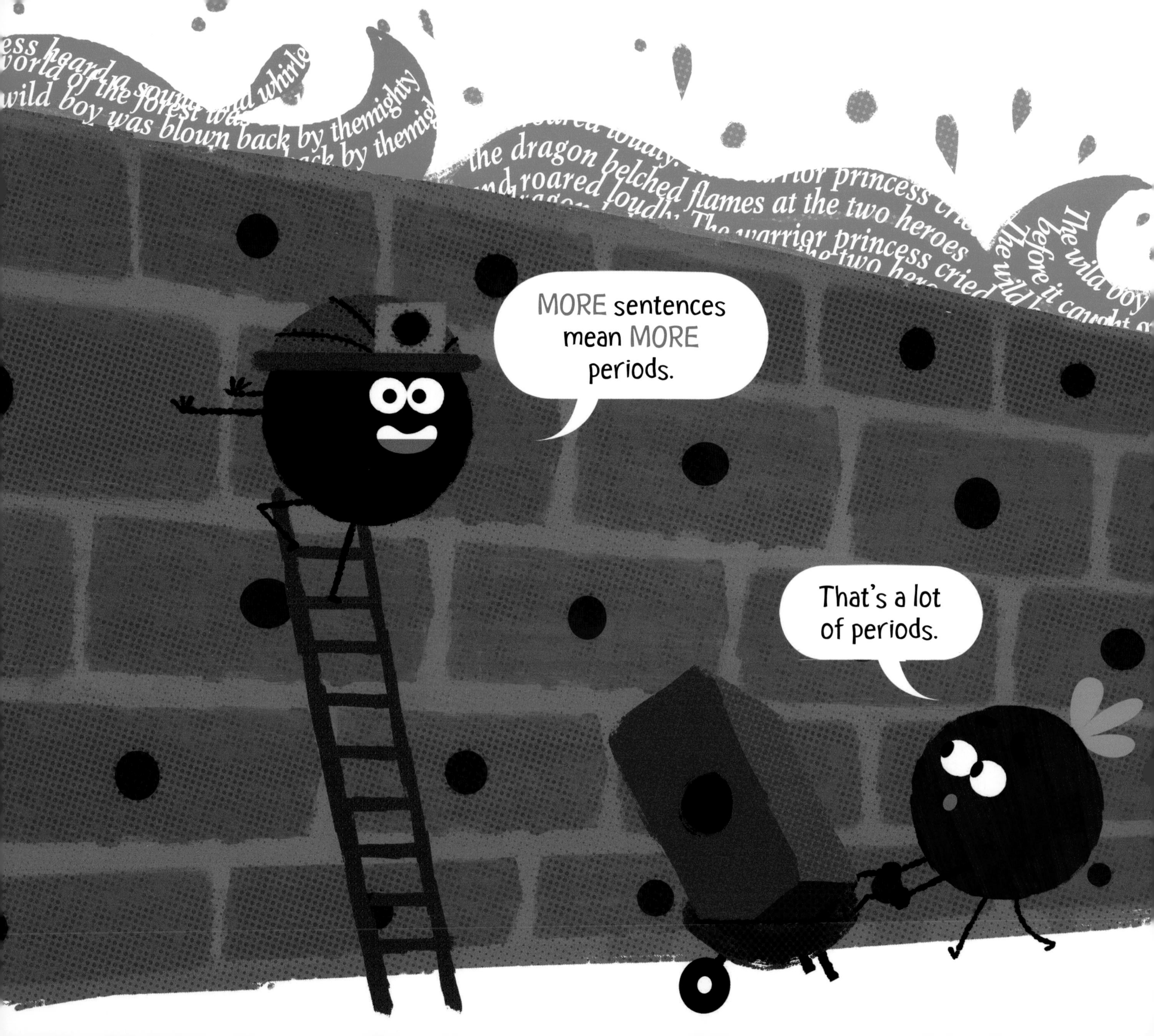
MORE sentences mean MORE periods.
That's a lot of periods.

oods jumped from his tree branch before it

the dragon belched

her fearsome

the wild boy raised

belched again

with wings

shadows shifted and shivered

The princess hung there

terrible bat-like w

The wings flapped

and flapped

by the

Without periods, sentences would look like this.

princess heard a sound and u
ragon belched flames at the ti
cess cried out the wild boy of t
it caught on fire the dragon
cess hung the creatu

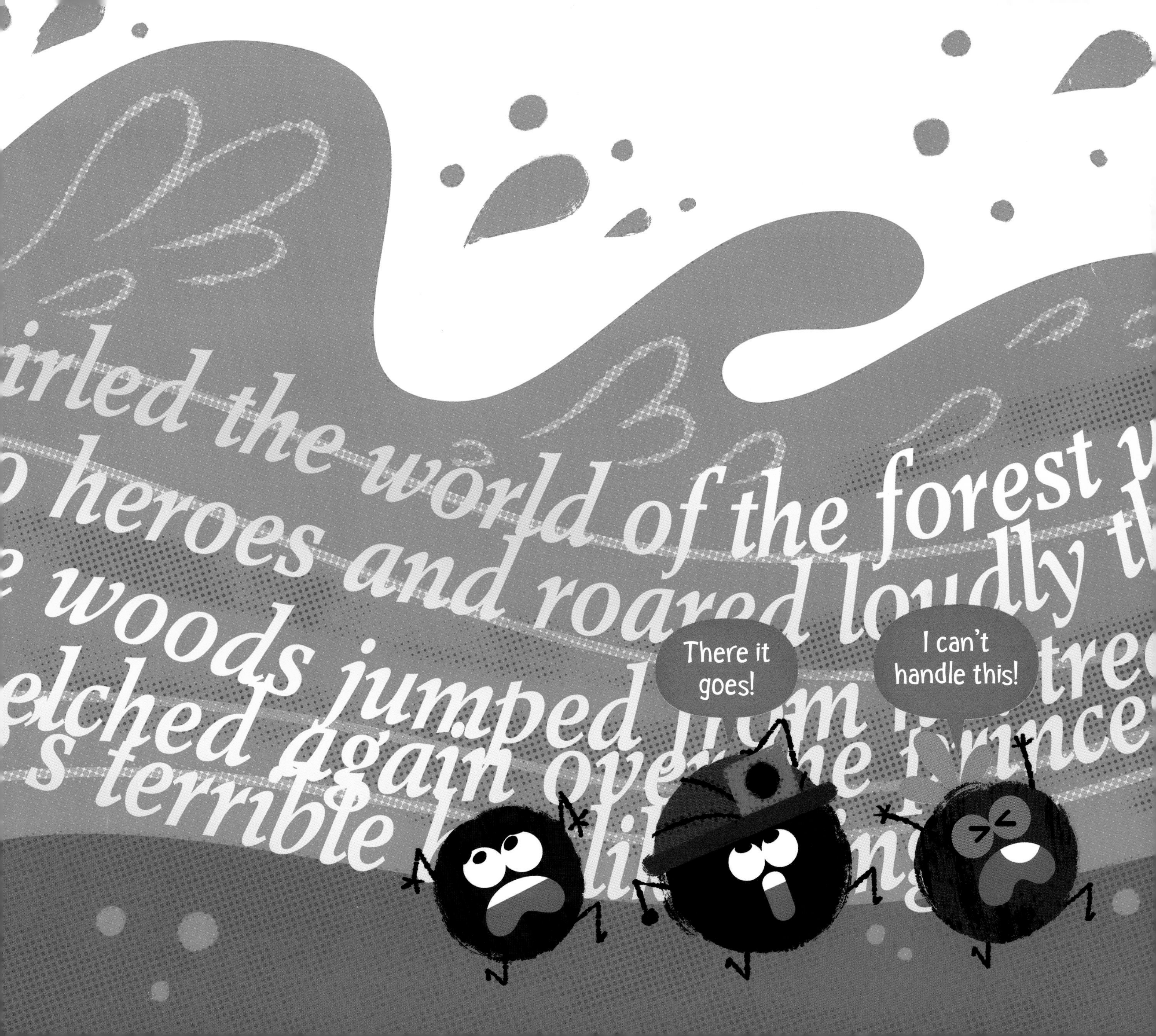
There it goes!
I can't handle this!

The creature's terrible bat-like wings

the wild boy was blown back by th

You will also find a period at the end of an abbreviation.
An abbreviation is a shorter way of writing a long word.

This is really helpful if you are squeezed for space.

JAN. FEBRUARY MARCH APRIL

UARY

MAY JUNE JULY AUGUST

SEPTEMBER OCTOBER NOVEMBER DECEMBER

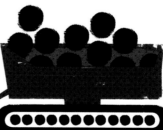

Here are more periods. Just in time.

Abbr.

Periods do
LOTS OF JOBS.

Mom's
Diner
Turn Rt. at
Next Exit

FREE
DENTAL
EXAMS

RIDE THE SURF
RELAX IN THE SUN

AT MT PLEASANT

DAZZLECON

GET YOUR
TICKETS

A.S.A.P.

There are so many other jobs,
we can't even squeeze them
all into this book.

Period.

POINTS ABOUT

Periods are found at the end of DECLARATIVE SENTENCES.
These sentences make a statement.

The wind
howled.

The shadows
danced.

Sometimes periods are used at the end of IMPERATIVE SENTENCES.
These sentences give a command.

Watch out for
more periods.

Periods are used in ABBREVIATIONS.
They help us shorten words.

You can use Oct.
to stand for
October.

Oct.~~ober~~

THE PERIOD

A period comes after a person's title but before his or her name.

Dr. Mason looks for periods in her paper.

To shorten a person's name, we may use his or her initials. We place a period after an initial.

R.J. signed his initials on the document.

We also use periods to help us tell time.

At 10 a.m. the bell will ring for recess.

ABOUT THE AUTHOR

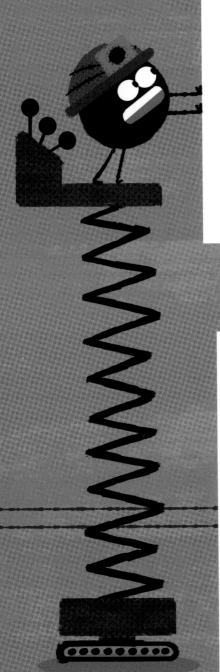

Michael Dahl is the author of more than 200 books for children and has won the AEP Distinguished Achievement Award three times for his nonfiction. He is the author of the bestselling *Bedtime for Batman* and *You're A Star, Wonder Woman!* picture books. He has written dozens of books of jokes, riddles, and puns. He likes to play with words. In grade school, he read the dictionary for fun. Really. And his favorite words are adverbs (*really* is an adverb, by the way).

ABOUT THE ILLUSTRATOR

Chris Garbutt hails from a family of tea-drinking hedgehogs that live deep in the magical hills of Yorkshire in the north of England. He has spent most of his time on this planet drawing cartoons and comics in London, Paris, and most recently Los Angeles, where he now creates funny pictures in exchange for cake. Most recently he has been the executive producer, show-runner, and art director of a new TV series he co-created at Nickelodeon called *Pinky Malinky*, which will be available on Netflix in 2019.

GLOSSARY

abbreviation—a shortened version of a word

capital letter—a larger version of a letter; used at the beginning of a sentence or as the first letter in a proper name

declarative sentence—a sentence that makes a statement

imperative sentence—a sentence that gives a command

initial—a letter that stands for a person's name

Looking for definitions?

READ MORE

Cleary, Brian P. *The Punctuation Station*. Minneapolis: Millbrook Press, 2010.

Collins, Terry. *Whatever Says Mark: Knowing and Using Punctuation*. Language on the Loose. North Mankato, Minn.: Picture Window Books, 2014.

Loewen, Nancy. *Frog. Frog? Frog!: Understanding Sentence Types*. Language on the Loose. North Mankato, Minn.: Picture Window Books, 2014.

CRITICAL THINKING QUESTIONS

1. What is a declarative sentence? Give an example.

2. What kind of sentence gives a command? Give an example.

3. What titles can be abbreviated? List three examples.

INTERNET SITES

Use FactHound to find Internet sites related to this book.

Visit *www.facthound.com*

Just type in this code: 9781515838609 and go.

 Check out projects, games and lots more at **www.capstonekids.com**

OTHER TITLES IN THE SERIES

Commas Say "Take a Break"
Exclamation Points Say "Wow!"
Question Marks Say "What?"

Editor: Shelly Lyons
Designer: Aruna Rangarajan and Hilary Wacholz
Creative Director: Nathan Gassman
Production Specialist: Tori Abraham
The illustrations in this book were created digitally.

Picture Window Books
are published by Capstone,
1710 Roe Crest Drive,
North Mankato, Minnesota 56003
www.mycapstone.com

Library of Congress Cataloging-in-Publication Data
is available on the Library of Congress website.
ISBN 978-1-5158-3860-9 (library hardcover)
ISBN 978-1-5158-4054-1 (paperback)
ISBN 978-1-5158-3864-7 (eBook PDF)

Summary: Periods say stop. They tell us when a
sentence ends, and they help us shorten words.
Follow along and learn all about hard-working
periods.

Printed and bound in the USA.
PA49